LOOK AND LEARN

WORDS FOR CATHOLIC KIDS

CASEY PAWELEK

2023 Fifth Printing
2022 First, Second, Third, and Fourth Printing

Look and Learn: Words for Catholic Kids

ISBN 978-1-64060-691-3

The Paraclete Press name and logo (dove on cross) are trademarks of Paraclete Press.

   Library of Congress Cataloging-in-Publication Data
Names: Pawelek, Casey, 1988- author.
Title: Look and learn : words for Catholic kids / by Casey Pawelek.
Description: Brewster, Massachusetts : Paraclete Press, [2022] | Audience:
   Ages 5 | Audience: Grades K-1 | Summary: "These illustrations with
   titles are a simple way to teach about faith and the love of God"—
   Provided by publisher.
Identifiers: LCCN 2021036310 | ISBN 9781640606913
Subjects: LCSH: Catholic Church—Pictorial works. | Catholic
   Church—Terminology—Juvenile literature. | Catholic Church—Juvenile
   literature.
Classification: LCC BX843 .P39 2022 | DDC 282—dc23
LC record available at https://lccn.loc.gov/2021036310

10 9 8 7 6 5

Published by Paraclete Press
Brewster, Massachusetts
www.paracletepress.com

Manufactured by Shenzhen Tianhong Printing Co. Ltd.
Printed October 2023, in Pinghu, Shenzhen, China
This product conforms to all applicable CPSIA standards.
Batch: 202310004STH

HELLO KIDS,

This book is full of pictures and words about our Catholic faith. If you don't know them already, don't worry! I am learning new things about the Church Jesus started all the time. As you explore the pages in this book, do not be afraid to ask questions. The Kingdom belongs to little ones just like you and the Holy Spirit is leading you on an amazing adventure!

Can you find some of these things in your home, in your church, and in your community? Once you do, it's your mission as a disciple to teach them to a friend. Jesus gave the Church, and all its fullness, to his apostles who passed it down. Now it is your turn to learn and go tell the Good News.

Let's go!

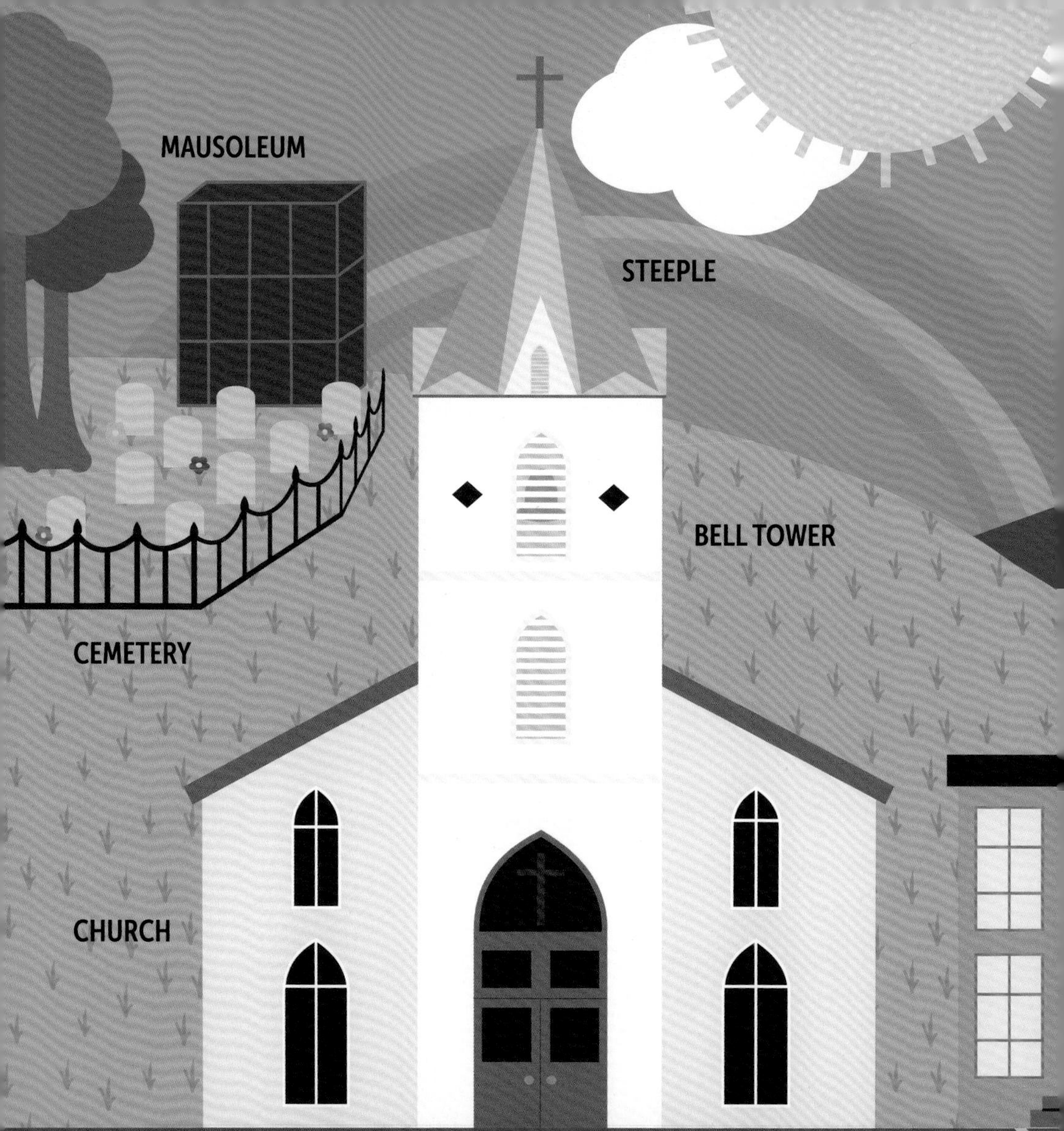

MAUSOLEUM

STEEPLE

BELL TOWER

CEMETERY

CHURCH

AROUND THE CHURCH

ADORATION
CHAPEL

STATIONS
OF THE CROSS

RECTORY

GROTTO

PARISH
OFFICES

PLAYGROUND

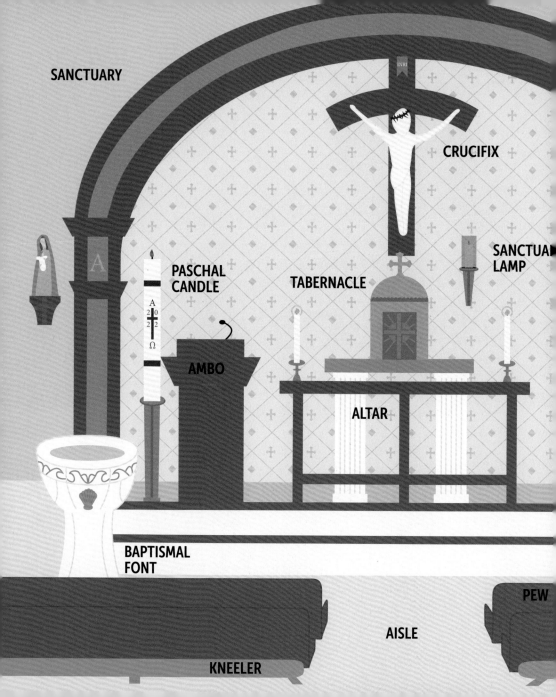

SANCTUARY

CRUCIFIX

SANCTUARY LAMP

PASCHAL CANDLE

TABERNACLE

A
2022
Ω

AMBO

ALTAR

BAPTISMAL FONT

PEW

AISLE

KNEELER

IN THE CHURCH

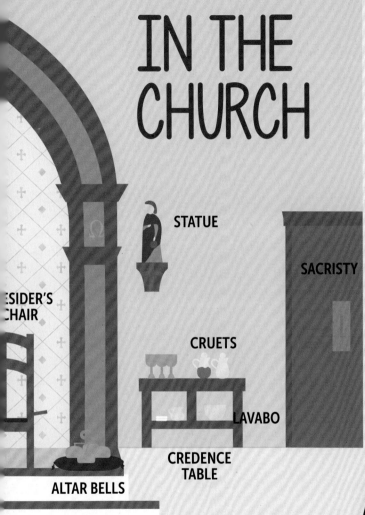

STATUE

PRESIDER'S CHAIR

CRUETS

LAVABO

CREDENCE TABLE

ALTAR BELLS

SACRISTY

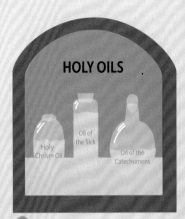

HOLY OILS

Holy Chrism Oil

Oil of the Sick

Oil of the Catechumens

STOUP

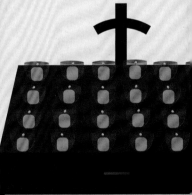

VOTIVE CANDLES

ROMAN MISSAL

CRUCIFIX

CANDLE

CHALICE

ON THE ALTAR

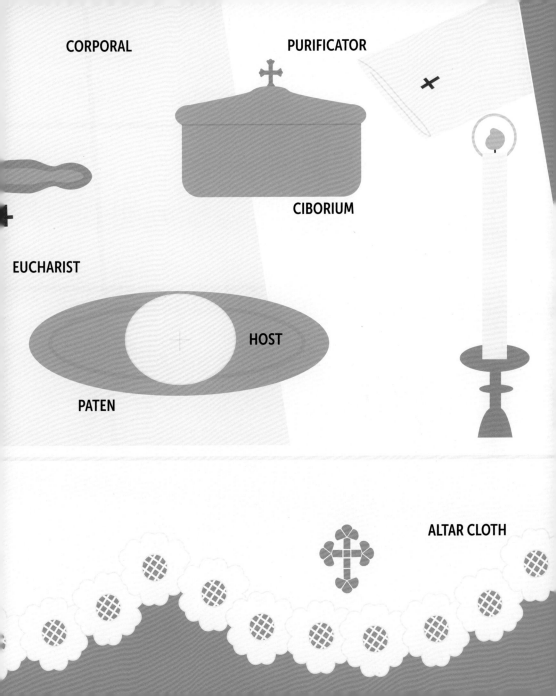

IN THE CHOIR

7
70
12
40

HYMN BOARD

ORGAN

PIANO

SHEET MUSIC

PEDALS

RESPONSORIAL PSALM

CANTOR

GUITAR

HYMNAL
SONG BOOK

MICROPHONE

MUSIC STAND

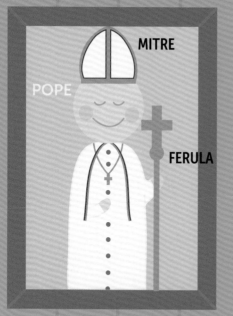

POPE — MITRE — FERULA

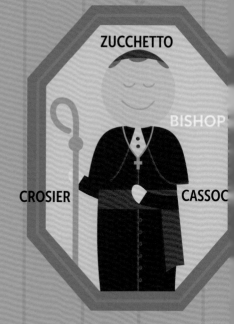

ZUCCHETTO — BISHOP — CROSIER — CASSOC

CARDINAL — BIRETTA — MOZETTA

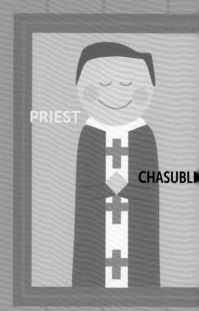

PRIEST — CHASUBL

PEOPLE OF THE CHURCH

DEACON

STOLE

ALB

NUN

VEIL

HABIT

LAITY

COLORS OF

PREPARATION

ADVENT

LENT

CELEBRATION

EASTER

CHRISTMAS

FEASTS OF THE BLESSED MOTHER

ANGELS & SAINTS NOT MARTYRED

THE LITURGY

GROWTH

ORDINARY TIME

JOY

LAETARE SUNDAY

GAUDETE SUNDAY

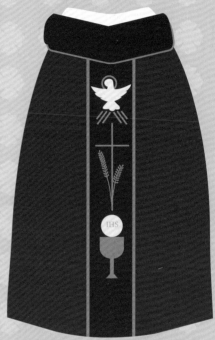

SACRIFICE

PALM SUNDAY

GOOD FRIDAY

PENTECOST

FEASTS OF APOSTLES AND MARTYRS

AROUND THE WORLD

CATHEDRALS & SHRINES

HOSPITALS

RELIEF MISSIONS

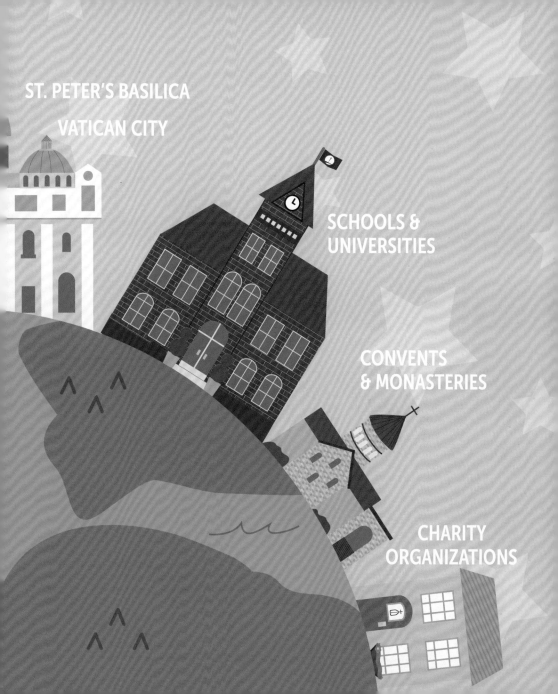

ST. PETER'S BASILICA

VATICAN CITY

SCHOOLS &
UNIVERSITIES

CONVENTS
& MONASTERIES

CHARITY
ORGANIZATIONS

IN THE HOME

DOMESTIC CHURCH

CRUCIFIX

SPIRITUAL APPS AND PODCASTS

LITANY

PRAYER CARDS

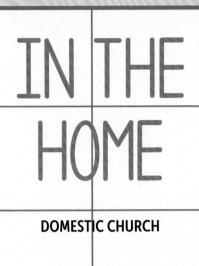

HOLY WATER

Holy Water

SACRED ART

us, I Trust in You

PILGRIMAGE

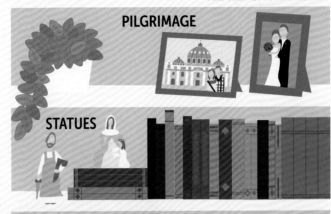

STATUES

ICON

RELIGIOUS BOOKS

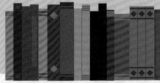

OLEMNITY
HOLY DAY
OBLIGATION

TRIDUUM

CATECHISM

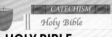

CATECHISM

Holy Bible

HOLY BIBLE

PRAYER SPACE

SACRAMENTS

BAPTISM

EUCHARIST

CONFIRMATION

INITIATION

RECONCILIATION

MATRIMONY

ANOINTING OF THE SICK

HOLY ORDERS

HEALING

SERVICE

CONFESSION

IN PERSONA CHRISTI

ABSOLUTION

PRIESTLY
STOLE

CONFESSOR

EXAMINATION OF
CONSCIENCE

GRILLE

CONFESSIONAL

ACT OF CONTRITION

Oh my God, I am heartily sorry for having offended you, and I detest of all my sins because of your just punishments, but most of all, because they offend you my God, who are all good and deserving of all my love. I firmly resolve, with the help of your grace, to sin no more and to avoid the near occasion of sin.
Amen.

PENANCE

 PENITENT

VIRTUES

PRUDENCE

JUSTICE

THEOLOGIC

HOP

FAITH

PRIDE

GREED

ENVY

WRATH

CARDINAL VIRTUES

FORTITUDE

TEMPERANCE

RTUES

CHARITY

VICES

LUST

GLUTTONY

SLOTH

OUR LADY

PONDER

MARIAN APPARITION

NEW ARK OF T
COVENANT

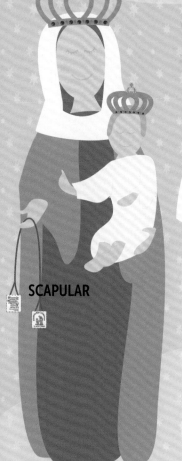

SCAPULAR

OUR LADY OF
MOUNT CARMEL

OUR LADY OF
LOURDES

OUR LADY OF
GUADALUPE

IMMACULATE
CONCEPTION

INTERCESSION

NEW EVE

OUR LADY OF THE
MIRACULOUS MEDAL

OUR LADY OF
FATIMA

OUR LADY OF
CHINA

THE HOLY ROSARY

Pray the Glory Be and the Fatima Prayer
Announce the Fifth Mystery
Pray the Our Father

Pray the Glory Be
and the Fatima Prayer
Pray the Hail Holy Queen
End with the Sign of the Cross

Pray the Glory Be
Announce First Mystery
Pray the Our Father

Pray the Our Father

Pray the Glory Be and the Fatima Prayer
Announce the Second Mystery
Pray the Our Father

Make the Sign of the Cross
and say the Apostles Creed

Hail Mary

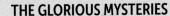

THE GLORIOUS MYSTERIES
Sunday & Wednesday
The Resurrection
The Ascension
The Descent of the Holy Spirit
The Assumption
The Crowning of Mary

**Pray the Glory Be and
the Fatima Prayer
Announce the Fourth Mystery
Pray the Our Father**

Hail Mary · Hail Mary · Hail Mary · Hail Mary · Hail Mary · Hail Mary · Hail Mary · Hail Mary · Hail Mary · Hail Mary · Hail Mary · Hail Mary · Hail Mary · Hail Mary

THE JOYFUL MYSTERIES
Monday & Saturday
The Annunciation
The Visitation
The Nativity
The Presentation
Finding Jesus in the
Temple

Hail Mary full of grace, the Lord is with thee.
Blessed art thou among women, and blessed
is the fruit of thy womb, Jesus. Holy Mary
Mother of God, pray for us sinners, now and at
the hour of our death.
Amen.

THE SORROWFUL MYSTERIES
Tuesday & Friday
The Agony in the Garden
The Scourging at the Pillar
The Crowning of Thorns
Jesus Takes Up His Cross
The Crucifixion

**Pray the Glory Be and
the Fatima Prayer
Announce the Third Mystery
Pray the Our Father**

Hail Mary · Hail Mary · Hail Mary · Hail Mary · Hail Mary · Hail Mary · Hail Mary

THE LUMINOUS MYSTERIES
Thursday
The Baptism of the Lord
The Wedding at Cana
The Proclamation of the Kingdom
The Transfiguration
The Institution of the Eucharist

OLD TESTAMENT

THE PENTATEUCH

Genesis
Exodus
Leviticus
Numbers
Deuteronomy
Joshua
Judges
Ruth

THE HISTORICAL BOOKS

1 Samuel
2 Samuel
1 Kings
2 Kings
1 Chronicles
2 Chronicles
Ezra
Nehemiah
Tobit
Judith
Esther
1 Maccabees
2 Maccabees

NEW TESTAMENT

THE GOSPELS

Matthew
Mark
Luke
John

THE

Acts
Romans
1 Corinthians
2 Corinthians
Galatians
Ephesians

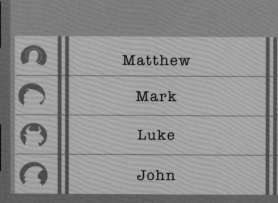

THE HOLY BIBLE

Proverbs

Ecclesiastes

Songs

Wisdom

Sirach

Isaiah

Jeremiah

Lamentations

Baruch

Ezekiel

Daniel

Hosea

Joel

Amos

Obadiah

Jonah

Micah

Nahum

Habakkuk

Zephaniah

Haggai

Zechariah

Malachi

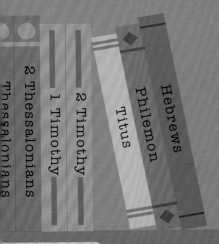

E WISDOM BOOKS

THE PROPHETIC BOOKS

2 Thessalonians

1 Thessalonians

2 Timothy

1 Timothy

Titus

Philemon

Hebrews

James

1 Peter

2 Peter

1 John

2 John

3 John

Jude

Revelation

AMENT LETTERS

THE CATHOLIC LETTERS

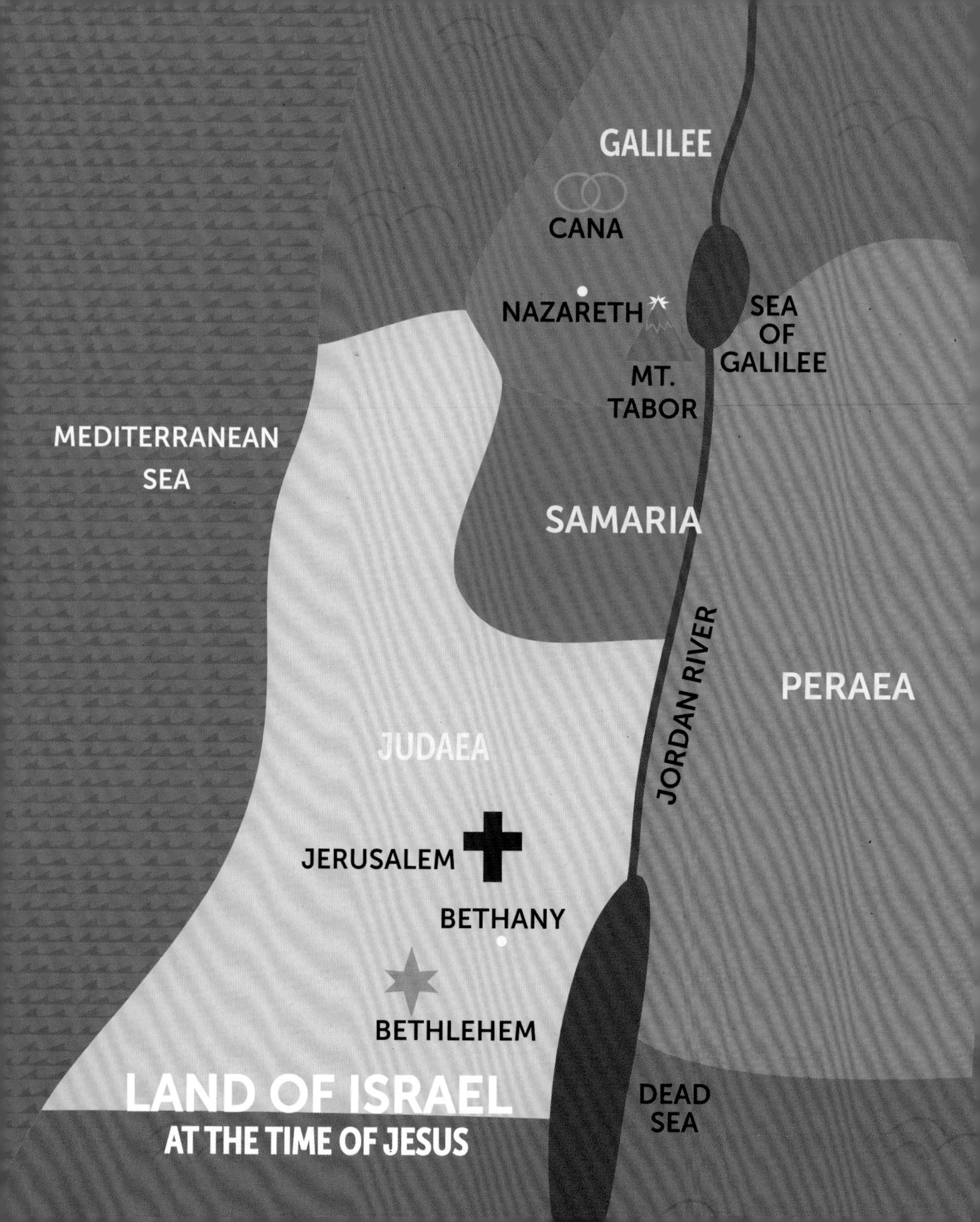

LAND OF ISRAEL
AT THE TIME OF JESUS

GALILEE

CANA

NAZARETH

SEA OF GALILEE

MT. TABOR

MEDITERRANEAN SEA

SAMARIA

JORDAN RIVER

PERAEA

JUDAEA

JERUSALEM

BETHANY

BETHLEHEM

DEAD SEA

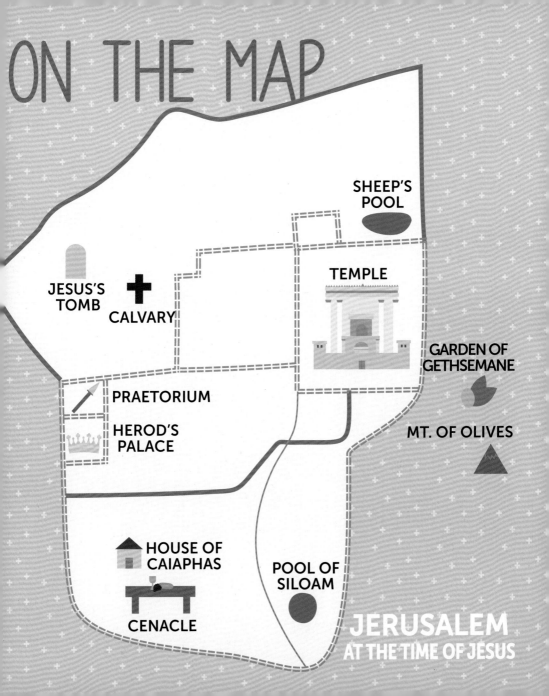

ON THE MAP

SHEEP'S POOL

JESUS'S TOMB

CALVARY

TEMPLE

GARDEN OF GETHSEMANE

MT. OF OLIVES

PRAETORIUM

HEROD'S PALACE

HOUSE OF CAIAPHAS

POOL OF SILOAM

CENACLE

JERUSALEM
AT THE TIME OF JESUS

GENEROSITY GENTLENESS FAITHFULNESS MODESTY SELF-CONTROL CHASTITY

FRUITS OF THE SPIRIT

A
Adoration

B
Bulletin

C
Canonization

D
Dogma

E
Epiclesis

F
Feast Day

G
Genuflect

H
Homily

I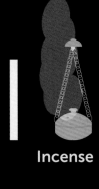
Incense

J
Jubilee

K
Kingdom

L
Liturgical Calendar

M
Mantilla

N
Novena

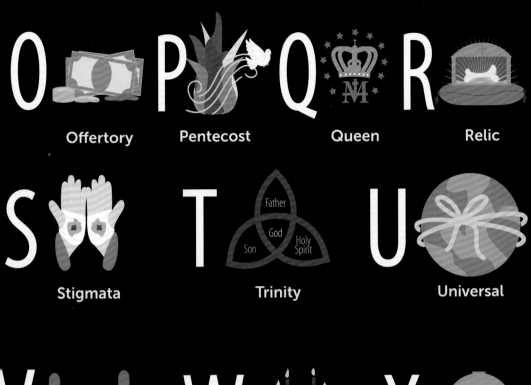

O Offertory

P Pentecost

Q Queen

R Relic

S Stigmata

T Trinity

Father
God
Son   Holy
       Spirit

U Universal

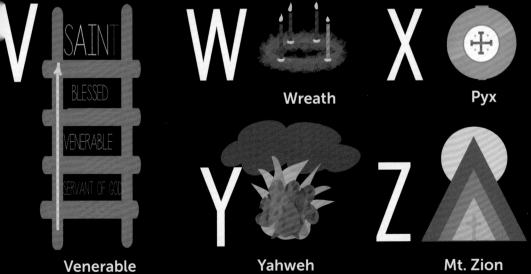

V Venerable

SAINT

BLESSED

VENERABLE

SERVANT OF GOD

W Wreath

X Pyx

Y Yahweh

Z Mt. Zion

KEEP GROWING

BIBLE STUDY

LOVE OF
NEIGHBOR

MISSION
TRIPS

CORPORAL &
SPIRITUAL WORKS
OF MERCY

DISCERNMENT

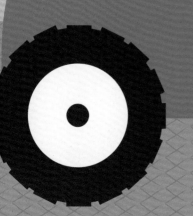

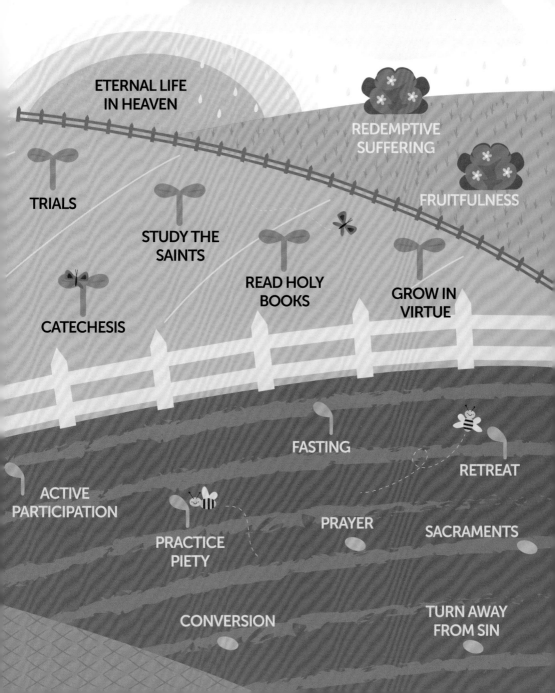

DEAR PARENTS & TEACHERS,

Thank you for exploring this book with your child! We have a great responsibility to pass on the faith to our children as we teach them about the love of God and nurture their relationship with Christ and His Church. As you turn the pages of this book, let your child lead you to the pictures and words that reach out to them. The Holy Spirit is at work! Our kids have a natural longing to know God and engage in the rich culture of our faith. It is not above their heads! As they learn the words in this book, watch how their confidence grows and see them actively participate. Jesus says, "Let the little ones come to me." So stand beside them, hold their hand, and lead by example as you continue on this journey of faith. May God bless you and your family!